Juan Mata

Published by **Creative Education** and **Creative Paperbacks**
P.O. Box 227, Mankato, Minnesota 56002
Creative Education and Creative Paperbacks are imprints of
The Creative Company
www.thecreativecompany.us

Design and production by **Christine Vanderbeek**
Art direction by **Rita Marshall**
Printed in the United States of America

Photographs by Alamy (Chronicle), Corbis (Colorsport, Daily Herald/
Mirrorpix, PHIL NOBLE/Reuters, PETER POWELL/epa, Reuters, DARREN
STAPLES/Reuters, Matt West/BPI), Getty Images (Popperfoto), photosinbox
.com, Shutterstock (anat chant, mooinblack, naipung, tele52)

Library of Congress Cataloging-in-Publication Data
Whiting, Jim.
Manchester United / Jim Whiting.
p. cm. — (Soccer stars)
Includes index.
Summary: An elementary introduction to the English soccer team
Manchester United, including a brief history since the team's 1878
founding, its main rivals, notable players, and Champions League titles.

ISBN 978-1-60818-803-1 (hardcover)
ISBN 978-1-62832-356-6 (pbk)
ISBN 978-1-56660-850-3 (eBook)
Manchester United (Soccer team)—History—Juvenile literature.
GV943.6.M3 W57 2016
796.33409427/33—dc23   2016000356

CCSS: RI.1.1, 2, 3, 4, 5, 6, 7; RI.2.1, 2, 4, 5, 6, 7, 10; RF.1.1, 3, 4; RF.2.3, 4

First Edition HC   9 8 7 6 5 4 3 2 1
First Edition PBK   9 8 7 6 5 4 3 2 1

Right: Daniel Welbeck

SOCCER STARS
MANCHESTER UNITED

Jim Whiting

CREATIVE EDUCATION · CREATIVE PAPERBACKS

MANCHESTER UNITED FAST FACTS

HOME ARENA: **Old Trafford**

TABLE OF CONTENTS

SOCCER STARS MANCHESTER UNITED

David Beckham

SOCCER STARS FRANK BARSON 1922–28

A former blacksmith, the midfielder was one of soccer's roughest players. Frank often told referees he was going to foul an opponent. Then he did exactly that.

Introducing Manchester United

MANCHESTER UNITED is one of the world's most famous soccer teams. Nicknamed "Red Devils" for their red jerseys, the team plays in England's Premier League. That is England's highest soccer league.

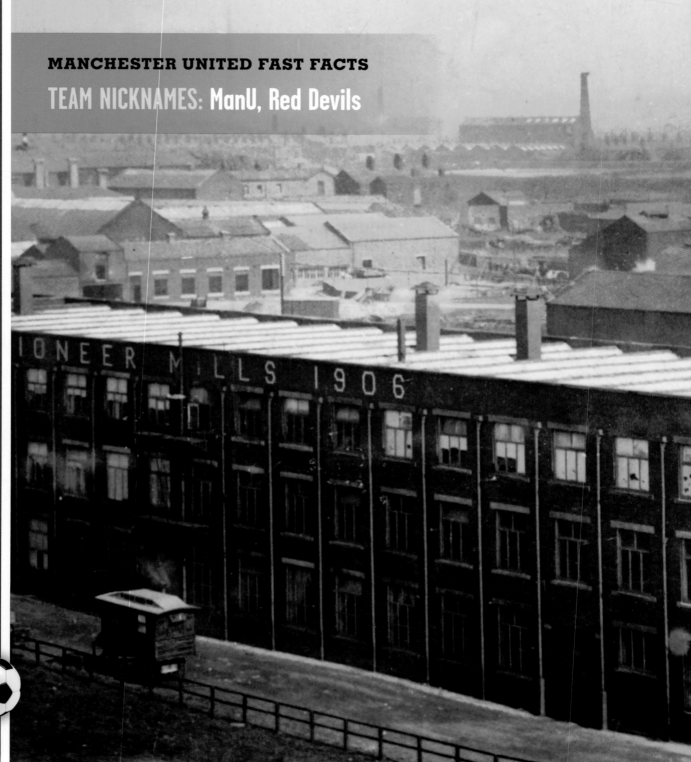

MANCHESTER UNITED FAST FACTS

TEAM NICKNAMES: ManU, Red Devils

Manchester

Manchester's Mills

THE TEAM PLAYS in the city of Manchester. Manchester was the center of the **Industrial Revolution**. It had a lot of **cotton mills**.

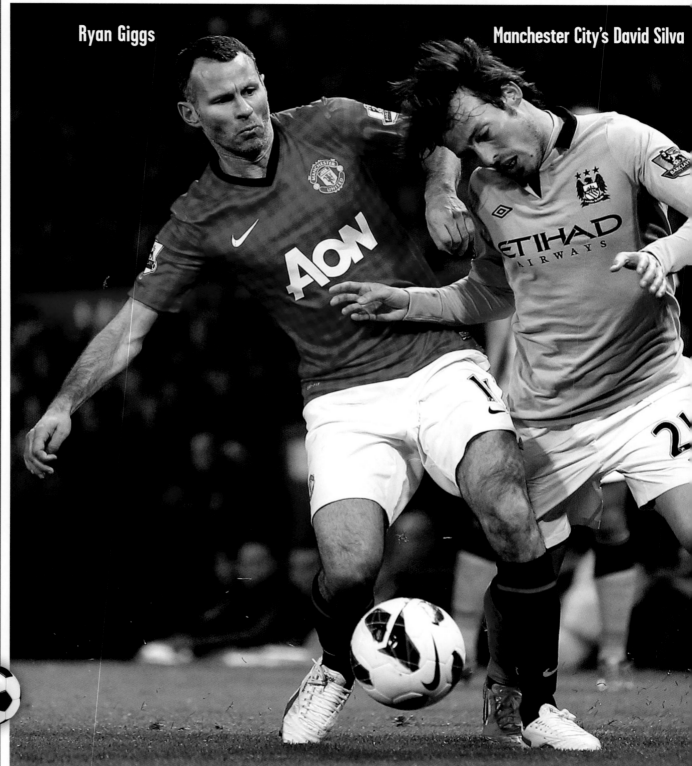

Ryan Giggs

Manchester City's David Silva

ManU vs. Liverpool

MANCHESTER CITY plays in Manchester, too. It is a strong <u>rival</u>. But ManU's biggest rival is Liverpool FC.

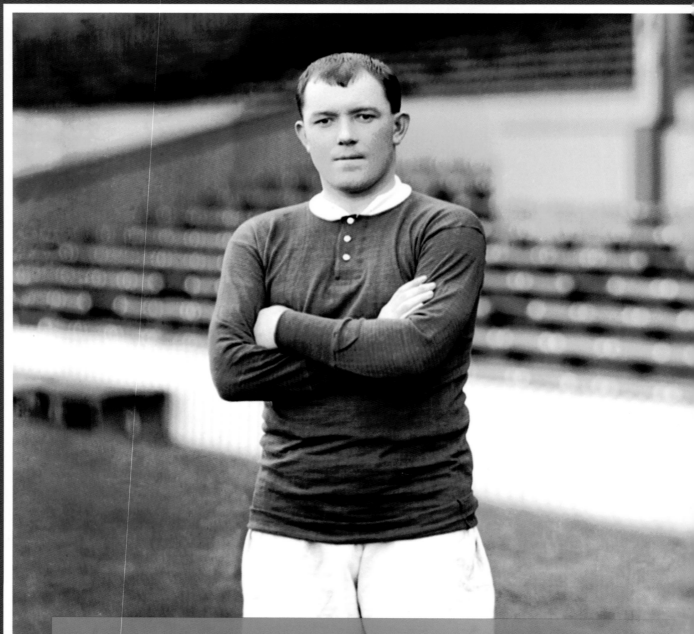

SOCCER STARS   ALEXANDER "SANDY" TURNBULL 1906–15

Sandy used his head to score the first goal at Old Trafford. He fought in World War I. He was part of the "footballer's battalion," with many other soccer players.

A Rough Start

RAILWAY WORKERS started the team in 1878. It was named Newton Heath Lancashire and Yorkshire Railway Football Club. The team joined the Football League 10 years later, but it didn't do well. Then a new owner took over in 1902. He changed the name to Manchester United. The team began to improve.

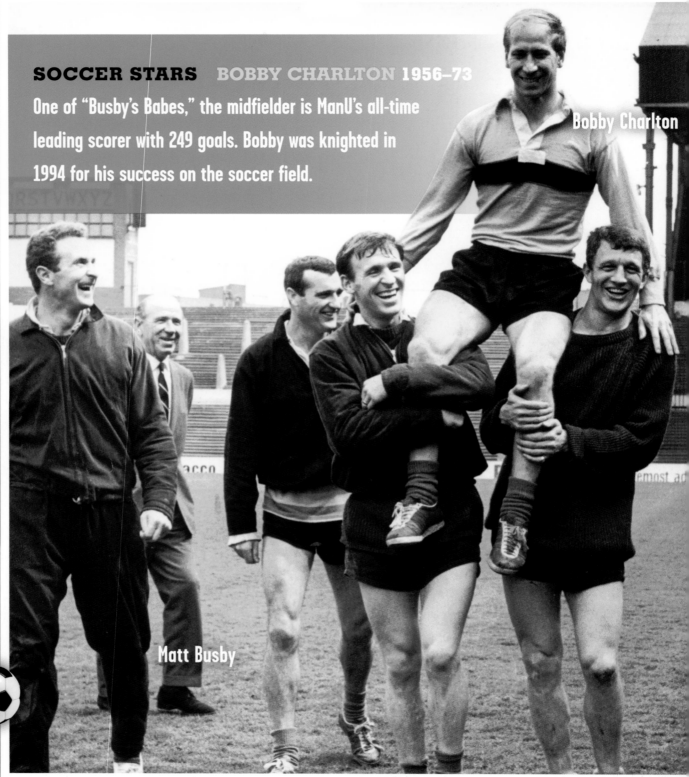

SOCCER STARS   BOBBY CHARLTON 1956–73

One of "Busby's Babes," the midfielder is ManU's all-time leading scorer with 249 goals. Bobby was knighted in 1994 for his success on the soccer field.

Bobby Charlton

Matt Busby

"Busby's Babes"

MANU WON Football League titles in 1908 and 1911. It didn't win another title until 1952, when manager Matt Busby had a lot of young players. They were known as "Busby's Babes." The Red Devils won back-to-back titles in 1956 and 1957.

George Best

A high-scoring forward, George was nicknamed the "Fifth Beatle" because of his long hair.

Overcoming Tragedy

TRAGEDY STRUCK the team in 1958. Eight players died in an airplane crash. Many others were hurt. The Red Devils had to rebuild. The team won two more titles in the 1960s, but then it went into a **slump**.

SOCCER STARS **WAYNE ROONEY 2004–present**

Wayne had a winning goal when he was just 16 years old. That made him the youngest goalscorer in Premier League history.

Premier Spot

TWENTY-TWO TEAMS split from the Football League to form the Premier League in 1992. The Red Devils controlled the new league! Players such as David Beckham, Wayne Rooney, Ryan Giggs, and Cristiano Ronaldo helped the team win 13 titles. They also won three **Champions League** titles. Red Devils fans expect the team to continue its winning ways!

SOCCER STARS   RYAN GIGGS 1990–2014
During his career, Ryan helped the Red Devils win 34 major trophies—more than any other player! He also holds the Premier League record for assists with 271.

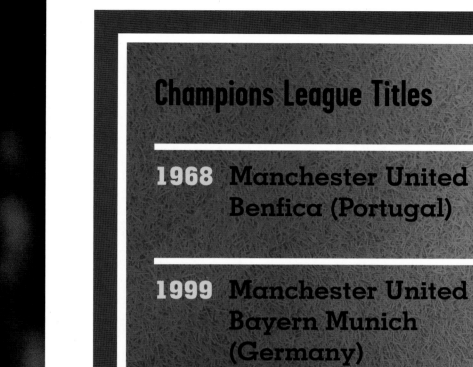

Champions League Titles

1968	Manchester United	**4**
	Benfica (Portugal)	**1**
1999	Manchester United	**2**
	Bayern Munich (Germany)	**1**
2008	Manchester United	**1**
	Chelsea (England)	**1**
	ManU won on penalty shootout (6–5)	

Read More

Cary, Gemma. *When I Grow up, I'm Going to Play for Manchester United*. Bath, U.K.: Hometown World, 2015.

Jökulsson, Illugi. *Manchester United: The Biggest and the Best*. New York: Abbeville Press, 2014.

Websites

HISTORY OF SOCCER FOR KIDS

http://www.ency123.com/2013/10/soccer-history-for-kids.html

This entertaining brief history of soccer is told in graphic form.

TOP 10 CHAMPIONS LEAGUE FINALS

http://www.sikids.com/photos/5201/top-10-champions-league-finals/1

Learn more about 10 notable Champions League finals matches.

Glossary

Champions League   an annual tournament among the top European soccer teams to see which one is best

cotton mills   factories where cotton was made into cloth

Industrial Revolution   a period in history when many people began working in factories in big cities

rival   a competitor

slump   a long period of losing or playing poorly

Note: Every effort has been made to ensure that the websites listed at left are suitable for children, that they have educational value, and that they contain no inappropriate material. However, because of the nature of the Internet, it is impossible to guarantee that these sites will remain active indefinitely or that their contents will not be altered.

Index